KATE GREENAWAY'S
Language of Flowers

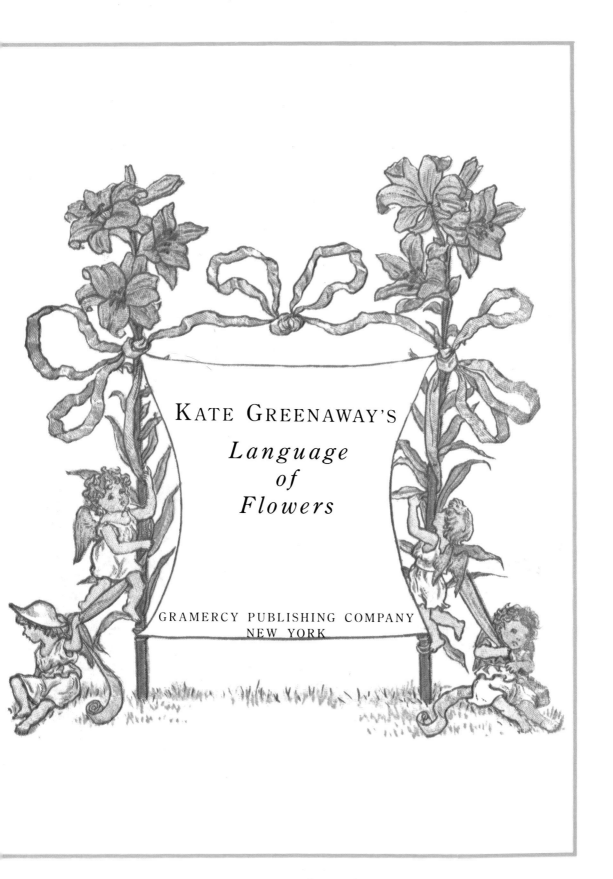

KATE GREENAWAY'S
*Language
of
Flowers*

GRAMERCY PUBLISHING COMPANY
NEW YORK

This edition, originally published as *Language of Flowers*, does not include the poems in the final section of the original edition.

This edition is published by Gramercy Publishing Company,
a division of Crown Publishers, Inc.
a b c d e f g h

GRAMERCY 1978 PRINTING
Manufactured in the United States of America

Library of Congress Cataloging in Publication Data

Greenaway, Kate, 1846-1901.
    Kate Greenaway's Language of flowers.

    Reprint of the 1884 ed. published by G. Routledge,
London, omitting the section, "Poetry on flowers."
      1. Greenaway, Kate, 1846-1901.   2. Flower language.
3. Flowers in art. I. Title. II. Title: Language
of flowers.
NC242.G7A4 1978a   741.9'42   78-14346
ISBN 0-517-26182-0

Abecedary	. . . .	*Volubility.*
Abatina	. . . .	*Fickleness.*
Acacia	. . . .	*Friendship.*
Acacia, Rose or White	. . . .	*Elegance.*
Acacia, Yellow	. . . .	*Secret love.*
Acanthus	. . . .	*The fine arts. Artifice.*
Acalia	. . . .	*Temperance.*
Achillea Millefolia	. . . .	*War.*
Aconite (Wolfsbane)	. . . .	*Misanthropy.*
Aconite, Crowfoot	. . . .	*Lustre.*
Adonis, Flos	. . . .	*Painful recollections.*
African Marigold	. . . .	*Vulgar minds.*
Agnus Castus	. . . .	*Coldness. Indifference.*
Agrimony	. . . .	*Thankfulness. Gratitude.*
Almond (Common)	. . . .	*Stupidity. Indiscretion.*

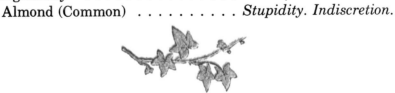

Almond (Flowering)	*Hope.*
Almond, Laurel	*Perfidy*
Allspice	*Compassion.*
Aloe	*Grief. Religious superstition.*
Althaea Frutex (Syrian Mallow)	*Persuasion.*
Alyssum (Sweet)	*Worth beyond beauty.*
Amaranth (Globe)	*Immortality. Unfading love.*
Amaranth (Cockscomb)	*Foppery. Affectation.*
Amaryllis	*Pride. Timidity. Splendid beauty.*
Ambrosia	*Love returned.*
American Cowslip	*Divine beauty.*
American Elm	*Patriotism.*
American Linden	*Matrimony.*
American Starwort	*Welcome to a stranger. Cheerfulness in old age.*
Amethys	*Admiration.*
Anemone (Zephyr Flower)	*Sickness. Expectation.*
Anemone (Garden)	*Forsaken.*
Angelica	*Inspiration.*
Angrec	*Royalty.*
Apple	*Temptation.*
Apple (Blossom)	*Preference. Fame speaks him great and good.*
Apple, Thorn	*Deceitful charms.*
Apocynum (Dog's Vane)	*Deceit.*
Arbor Vitae	*Unchanging Friendship. Live for me.*
Arum (Wake Robin)	*Ardour.*
Ash-leaved Trumpet Flower . . .	*Separation.*
Ash Tree	*Grandeur.*
Aspen Tree	*Lamentation.*
Aster (China)	*Variety. Afterthought.*
Asphodel	*My regrets follow you to the grave.*
Auricula	*Painting.*
Auricula, Scarlet	*Avarice.*
Austurtium	*Splendour.*
Azalea	*Temperance.*

Bachelor's Buttons . . . . *Celibacy.*

Balm . . . . *Sympathy.*

Balm, Gentle . . . . *Pleasantry.*

Balm of Gilead . . . . *Cure. Relief.*

Balsam, Red . . . . *Touch me not. Impatient resolves.*

Balsam, Yellow . . . . *Impatience.*

Barberry . . . . *Sourness of temper.*

Barberry Tree . . . . *Sharpness.*

Basil . . . . *Hatred.*

Bay Leaf . . . . *I change but in death.*

Bay (Rose) Rhododendron . . . *Danger. Beware.*

Bay Tree . . . . *Glory.*

Bay Wreath . . . . *Reward of merit.*

Bearded Crepis . . . . *Protection.*

Beech Tree . . . . *Prosperity.*

Bee Orchis . . . . *Industry.*

Bee Ophrys . . . . *Error.*

Belladonna . . . . *Silence.*

Bell Flower, Pyramidal . . . . . *Constancy.*

Bell Flower (small white) . . . . *Gratitude.*

Belvedere	*I declare against you.*
Betony	*Surprise.*
Bilberry	*Treachery.*
Bindweed, Great	*Insinuation.*
Bindweed, Small	*Humility.*
Birch	*Meekness.*
Birdsfoot Trefoil	*Revenge.*
Bittersweet; Nightshade	*Truth.*
Black Poplar	*Courage.*
Blackthorn	*Difficulty.*
Bladder Nut Tree	*Frivolity. Amusement.*
Bluebottle (Centaury)	*Delicacy.*
Bluebell	*Constancy.*
Blue-flowered Greek Valerian	*Rupture.*
Borus Henricus	*Goodness.*
Borage	*Bluntness.*
Box Tree	*Stoicism.*
Bramble	*Lowliness. Envy. Remorse.*
Branch of Currants	*You please all.*
Branch of Thorns	*Severity. Rigour.*
Bridal Rose	*Happy love.*
Broom	*Humility. Neatness.*
Buckbean	*Calm repose.*
Bud of White Rose	*Heart ignorant of love.*
Bugloss	*Falsehood.*
Bulrush	*Indiscretion. Docility.*
Bundle of Reeds, with their Panicles	*Music.*
Burdock	*Importunity. Touch me not.*
Buttercup (Kingcup)	*Ingratitude. Childishness.*
Butterfly Orchis	*Gaiety.*
Butterfly Weed	*Let me go.*

Cabbage	*Profit.*
Cacalia	*Adulation.*
Cactus	*Warmth.*
Calla Æthiopica	*Magnificent Beauty.*
Calycanthus	*Benevolence.*
Camellia Japonica, Red	*Unpretending excellence.*
Camellia Japonica, White	*Perfected loveliness.*
Camomile	*Energy in adversity.*
Canary Grass	*Perserverance.*
Candytuft	*Indifference.*
Canterbury Bell	*Acknowledgement.*
Cape Jasmine	*I'm too happy.*
Cardamine	*Paternal error.*
Carnation, Deep Red	*Alas! for my poor heart.*
Carnation, Striped	*Refusal.*
Carnation, Yellow	*Disdain.*

Cardinal Flower	*Distinction.*
Catchfly	*Snare.*
Catchfly, Red	*Youthful love.*
Catchfly, White	*Betrayed.*
Cedar	*Strength.*
Cedar of Lebanon	*Incorruptible.*
Cedar Leaf	*I live for thee.*
Celandine (Lesser)	*Joys to come.*
Cereus (Creeping)	*Modest genius.*
Centaury	*Delicacy.*
Champignon	*Suspicion.*
Chequered Fritillary	*Persecution.*
Cherry Tree	*Good education.*
Cherry Tree, White	*Deception.*
Chesnut Tree	*Do me justice. Luxury.*
Chickweed	*Rendezvous.*
Chicory	*Frugality.*
China Aster	*Variety.*
China Aster, Double	*I partake your sentiments.*
China Aster, Single	*I will think of it.*
China or Indian Pink	*Aversion.*
China Rose	*Beauty always new.*
Chinese Chrysanthemum	*Cheerfulness under adversity.*
Christmas Rose	*Relieve my anxiety.*
Chrysanthemum, Red	*I love.*
Chrysanthemum, White	*Truth.*
Chrysanthemum, Yellow	*Slighted love.*
Cinquefoil	*Maternal affection.*
Circæa	*Spell.*
Cistus, or Rock Rose	*Popular favour.*
Cistus, Gum	*I shall die to-morrow.*
Citron	*Ill-natured beauty.*
Clematis	*Mental beauty.*
Clematis, Evergreen	*Poverty.*
Clotbur	*Rudeness. Pertinacity.*
Cloves	*Dignity.*
Clover, Four-leaved	*Be mine.*
Clover, Red	*Industry.*
Clover, White	*Think of me.*
Cobæa	*Gossip.*
Cockscomb Amaranth	*Foppery. Affectation. Singularity.*

Colchicum, or Meadow Saffron . . *My best days are past.*
Coltsfoot . . . . *Justice shall be done.*
Columbine . . . . *Folly.*
Columbine, Purple . . . . *Resolved to win.*
Columbine, Red . . . . *Anxious and trembling.*
Convolvulus . . . . *Bonds.*
Convolvulus, Blue (Minor) . . . . *Repose. Night.*
Convolvulus, Major . . . . *Extinguished hopes.*
Convolvulus, Pink . . . . *Worth sustained by judicious and tender affection.*
Corchorus . . . . *Impatient of absence.*
Coreopsis . . . . *Always cheerful.*
Coreopsis Arkansa . . . . *Love at first sight.*
Coriander . . . . *Hidden worth.*
Corn . . . . *Riches.*
Corn, Broken . . . . *Quarrel.*
Corn Straw . . . . *Agreement.*
Corn Bottle . . . . *Delicacy.*
Corn Cockle . . . . *Gentility.*
Cornel Tree . . . . *Duration.*
Coronella . . . . *Success crown your wishes.*
Cowslip . . . . *Pensiveness. Winning grace.*
Cowslip, American . . . . *Divine beauty. You are my divinity.*
Cranberry . . . . *Cure for heartache.*
Creeping Cereus . . . . *Horror.*
Cress . . . . *Stability. Power.*
Crocus . . . . *Abuse not.*
Crocus, Spring . . . . *Youthful gladness.*
Crocus, Saffron . . . . *Mirth.*
Crown Imperial . . . . *Majesty. Power.*

Crowsbill	*Envy.*
Crowfoot	*Ingratitude.*
Crowfoot (Aconite-leaved)	*Lustre.*
Cuckoo Plant	*Ardour.*
Cudweed, American	*Unceasing remembrance.*
Currant	*Thy frown will kill me.*
Cuscuta	*Meanness.*
Cyclamen	*Diffidence.*
Cypress	*Death. Mourning.*

Daffodil . . . . *Regard.*
Dahlia . . . . *Instability.*
Daisy . . . . *Innocence.*
Daisy, Garden . . . . *I share your sentiments*
Daisy, Michaelmas . . . . . *Farewell.*
Daisy, Party-coloured . . . . *Beauty.*
Daisy, Wild . . . . *I will think of it.*
Damask Rose . . . . *Brilliant complexion.*
Dandelion . . . . *Rustic oracle.*
Daphne Odora . . . . *Painting the lily.*
Darnel (Ray grass) . . . . . . *Vice.*
Dead Leaves . . . . *Sadness.*
Dew Plant . . . . *A Serenade.*
Dittany of Crete . . . . *Birth.*
Dittany of Crete, White . . . *Passion.*
Dock . . . . *Patience.*
Dodder of Thyme . . . . *Baseness.*
Dogsbane . . . . *Deceit. Falsehood.*
Dogwood . . . . *Durability.*
Dragon Plant . . . . *Snare.*
Dragonwort . . . . *Horror.*
Dried Flax . . . . *Utility.*

Ebony Tree	*Blackness.*
Eglantine (Sweetbrier)	*Poetry. I wound to heal.*
Elder	*Zealousness.*
Elm	*Dignity.*
Enchanter's Nightshade	*Witchcraft. Sorcery.*
Endive	*Frugality.*
Eupatorium	*Delay.*
Everflowering Candytuft	*Indifference.*
Evergreen Clematis	*Poverty.*
Evergreen Thorn	*Solace in adversity.*
Everlasting	*Never-ceasing remembrance.*
Everlasting Pea	*Lasting pleasure.*
Fennel	*Worthy all praise. Strength.*

Fern . . . . *Fascination.*
Ficoides, Ice Plant . . . . *Your looks freeze me.*
Fig . . . . *Argument.*
Fig Marigold . . . . *Idleness.*
Fig Tree . . . . *Prolific.*
Filbert . . . . *Reconciliation.*
Fir . . . . *Time.*
Fir Tree . . . . *Elevation.*
Flax . . . . *Domestic Industry. Fate. I*
feel your kindness.
Flax-leaved Goldy-locks . . . . . *Tardiness.*
Fleur-de-Lis . . . . *Flame. I burn.*
Fleur-de-Luce . . . . *Fire.*
Flowering Fern . . . . *Reverie.*
Flowering Reed . . . . *Confidence in Heaven.*
Flower-of-an-Hour . . . . *Delicate beauty.*
Fly Orchis . . . . *Error.*

Flytrap	*Deceit.*
Fool's Parsley	*Silliness.*
Forget Me Not	*True love. Forget me not.*
Foxglove	*Insincerity.*
Foxtail Grass	*Sporting.*
French Honeysuckle	*Rustic beauty.*
French Marigold	*Jealousy.*
French Willow	*Bravery and humanity.*
Frog Ophrys	*Disgust.*
Fuller's Teasel	*Misanthropy.*
Fumitory	*Spleen.*
Fuchsia, Scarlet	*Taste.*

Garden Anemone	Forsaken.
Garden Chervil	Sincerity.
Garden Daisy	I partake your sentiments.
Garden Marigold	Uneasiness.
Garden Ranunculus	You are rich in attractions.
Garden Sage	Esteem.
Garland of Roses	Reward of virtue.
Germander Speedwell	Facility.
Geranium, Dark	Melancholy.
Geranium, Ivy	Bridal favour.
Geranium, Lemon	Unexpected meeting.
Geranium, Nutmeg	Expected meeting.
Geranium, Oak-leaved	True friendship.
Geranium, Pencilled	Ingenuity.
Geranium, Rose-scented	Preference.
Geranium, Scarlet	Comforting. Stupidity.
Geranium, Silver-leaved	Recall.
Geranium, Wild	Steadfast piety.

Gillyflower	. . . .	*Bonds of affection.*
Glory Flower	. . . .	*Glorious beauty.*
Goat's Rue	. . . .	*Reason.*
Golden Rod	. . . .	*Precaution.*
Gooseberry	. . . .	*Anticipation.*
Gourd	. . . .	*Extent, Bulk.*
Grape, Wild	. . . .	*Charity.*
Grass	. . . .	*Submission. Utility.*
Guelder Rose	. . . .	*Winter. Age.*

Hand Flower Tree	*Warning.*
Harebell	*Submission. Grief.*
Hawkweed	*Quicksightedness.*
Hawthorn	*Hope.*
Hazel	*Reconciliation.*
Heath	*Solitude.*
Helenium	*Tears.*
Heliotrope	*Devotion. Faithfulness.*
Hellebore	*Scandal. Calumny.*
Helmet Flower (Monkshood)	*Knight-errantry.*
Hemlock	*You will be my death.*
Hemp	*Fate.*
Henbane	*Imperfection.*
Hepatica	*Confidence.*
Hibiscus	*Delicate beauty.*
Holly	*Foresight.*
Holly Herb	*Enchantment.*
Hollyhock	*Ambition. Fecundity.*
Honesty	*Honesty. Fascination.*

Honey Flower	*Love sweet and secret.*
Honeysuckle	*Generous and devoted affection.*
Honeysuckle Coral	*The colour of my fate.*
Honeysuckle (French)	*Rustic beauty.*
Hop	*Injustice.*
Hornbeam	*Ornament.*
Horse Chesnut	*Luxury.*
Hortensia	*You are cold.*
Houseleek	*Vivacity. Domestic industry.*
Houstonia	*Content.*
Hoya	*Sculpture.*
Humble Plant	*Despondency.*
Hundred-leaved Rose	*Dignity of mind.*
Hyacinth	*Sport. Game. Play.*
Hyacinth, White	*Unobtrusive loveliness.*
Hydrangea	*A boaster. Heartlessness.*
Hyssop	*Cleanliness.*

Iceland Moss	. . . .	*Health.*
Ice Plant	. . . .	*Your looks freeze me.*
Imperial Montague	. . . .	*Power.*
Indian Cress	. . . .	*Warlike trophy.*
Indian Jasmine (Ipomœa)	. . . .	*Attachment.*
Indian Pink (Double)	. . . .	*Always lovely.*
Indian Plum	. . . .	*Privation.*
Iris	. . . .	*Message.*
Iris, German	. . . .	*Flame.*
Ivy	. . . .	*Fidelity. Marriage.*
Ivy, Sprig of, with tendrils	. . . .	*Assiduous to please.*

Jacob's Ladder	*Come down.*
Japan Rose	*Beauty is your only attraction.*
Jasmine	*Amiability.*
Jasmine, Cape	*Transport of joy.*
Jasmine, Carolina	*Separation.*
Jasmine, Indian	*I attach myself to you.*
Jasmine, Spanish	*Sensuality.*
Jasmine, Yellow	*Grace and elegance.*
Jonquil	*I desire a return of affection.*
Judas Tree	*Unbelief. Betrayal.*
Juniper	*Succour. Protection.*
Justicia	*The perfection of female loveliness.*

Kennedia . . . . *Mental Beauty.*
King-cups . . . . *Desire of Riches.*

Laburnum	Forsaken. Pensive Beauty.
Lady's Slipper	Capricious Beauty. Win me and wear me.
Lagerstræmia, Indian	Eloquence.
Lantana	Rigour.
Larch	Audacity. Boldness.
Larkspur	Lightness. Levity.
Larkspur, Pink	Fickleness.
Larkspur, Purple	Haughtiness.
Laurel	Glory.
Laurel, Common, in flower	Perfidy.
Laurel, Ground	Perseverance.
Laurel, Mountain	Ambition.
Laurel-leaved Magnolia	Dignity.
Laurestina	A token. I die if neglected.
Lavender	Distrust.
Leaves (dead)	Melancholy.
Lemon	Zest.
Lemon Blossoms	Fidelity in love.
Lettuce	Cold-heartedness.
Lichen	Dejection. Solitude.

Lilac, Field . . . . *Humility.*
Lilac, Purple . . . . *First emotions of love.*
Lilac, White . . . . *Youthful Innocence.*
Lily, Day . . . . *Coquetry.*
Lily, Imperial . . . . *Majesty.*
Lily, White . . . . *Purity. Sweetness.*
Lily, Yellow . . . . *Falsehood. Gaiety.*
Lily of the Valley . . . . *Return of happiness.*
Linden or Lime Trees . . . . *Conjugal love.*
Lint . . . . *I feel my obligations.*
Live Oak . . . . *Liberty.*
Liverwort . . . . *Confidence.*
Licorice, Wild . . . . *I declare against you.*
Lobelia . . . . *Malevolence.*
Locust Tree . . . . *Elegance.*
Locust Tree (green) . . . . *Affection beyond the grave.*
London Pride . . . . *Frivolity.*
Lote Tree . . . . *Concord.*
Lotus . . . . *Eloquence.*
Lotus Flower . . . . *Estranged love.*
Lotus Leaf . . . . *Recantation.*
Love in a Mist . . . . *Perplexity.*
Love lies Bleeding . . . . *Hopeless, not heartless.*
Lucern . . . . *Life.*
Lupine . . . . *Voraciousness. Imagination.*

Madder	*Calumny.*
Magnolia	*Love of Nature.*
Magnolia, Swamp	*Perseverance.*
Mallow	*Mildness.*
Mallow, Marsh	*Beneficence.*
Mallow, Syrian	*Consumed by love.*
Mallow, Venetian	*Delicate beauty.*
Manchineal Tree	*Falsehood.*
Mandrake	*Horror.*
Maple	*Reserve.*
Marigold	*Grief.*
Marigold, African	*Vulgar minds.*
Marigold, French	*Jealousy.*
Marigold, Prophetic	*Prediction.*
Marigold and Cypress	*Despair.*
Marjoram	*Blushes.*
Marvel of Peru	*Timidity.*

Meadow Lychnis	*Wit.*
Meadow Saffron	*My best days are past.*
Meadowsweet	*Uselessness.*
Mercury	*Goodness.*
Mesembryanthemum	*Idleness.*
Mezereon	*Desire to please.*
Michaelmas Daisy	*Afterthought.*
Mignionette	*Your qualities surpass your charms.*
Milfoil	*War.*
Milvetch	*Your presence softens my pains.*
Milkwort	*Hermitage.*
Mimosa (Sensitive Plant)	*Sensitiveness.*
Mint	*Virtue.*
Mistletoe	*I surmount difficulties.*
Mock Orange	*Counterfeit.*
Monkshood (Helmet Flower) . .	*Chivalry. Knight-errantry.*
Moonwort	*Forgetfulness.*
Morning Glory	*Affectation.*
Moschatel	*Weakness.*
Moss	*Maternal love.*
Mosses	*Ennui.*
Mossy Saxifrage	*Affection.*
Motherwort	*Concealed love.*
Mountain Ash	*Prudence.*
Mourning Bride	*Unfortunate attachment. I have lost all.*
Mouse-eared Chickweed	*Ingenuous simplicity.*
Mouse-eared Scorpion Grass . . .	*Forget me not.*
Moving Plant	*Agitation.*
Mudwort	*Tranquillity.*
Mugwort	*Happiness.*
Mulberry Tree (Black)	*I shall not survive you.*
Mulberry Tree (White)	*Wisdom.*
Mushroom	*Suspicion.*
Musk Plant	*Weakness.*
Mustard Seed	*Indifference.*
Myrobalan	*Privation.*
Myrrh	*Gladness.*
Myrtle	*Love.*

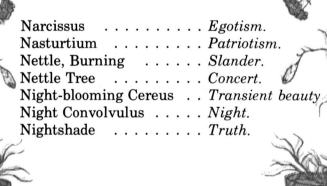

Narcissus	. . . .	*Egotism.*
Nasturtium	. . . .	*Patriotism.*
Nettle, Burning	. . . . .	*Slander.*
Nettle Tree	. . . .	*Concert.*
Night-blooming Cereus	. .	*Transient beauty*
Night Convolvulus	. . . . .	*Night.*
Nightshade	. . . .	*Truth.*

Oak Leaves	*Bravery.*
Oak Tree	*Hospitality.*
Oak (White)	*Independence.*
Oats	*The witching soul of music.*
Oleander	*Beware.*
Olive	*Peace.*
Orange Blossoms	*Your purity equals your loveliness.*
Orange Flowers	*Chastity. Bridal festivities.*
Orange Tree	*Generosity.*
Orchis	*A Belle.*
Osier	*Frankness.*
Osmunda	*Dreams.*
Ox Eye	*Patience.*

Palm	*Victory.*
Pansy	*Thoughts.*
Parsley	*Festivity.*
Pasque Flower	*You have no claims.*
Passion Flower	*Religious superstition.*
Patience Dock	*Patience.*
Pea, Everlasting	*An appointed meeting.*
	Lasting Pleasure.
Pea, Sweet	*Departure.*
Peach	*Your qualities, like your*
	charms, are unequalled.
Peach Blossom	*I am your captive.*
Pear	*Affection.*
Pear Tree	*Comfort.*
Pennyroyal	*Flee away.*
Peony	*Shame, Bashfulness.*
Peppermint	*Warmth of feeling.*
Periwinkle, Blue	*Early friendship.*
Periwinkle, White	*Pleasures of memory.*
Persicaria	*Restoration.*

Persimon	*Bury me amid Nature's beauties.*
Peruvian Heliotrope	*Devotion.*
Pheasant's Eye	*Remembrance.*
Phlox	*Unanimity.*
Pigeon Berry	*Indifference.*
Pimpernel	*Change. Assignation.*
Pine	*Pity.*
Pine-apple	*You are perfect.*
Pine, Pitch	*Philosophy.*
Pine, Spruce	*Hope in adversity.*
Pink	*Boldness.*
Pink, Carnation	*Woman's love.*
Pink, Indian, Double	*Always lovely.*
Pink, Indian, Single	*Aversion.*
Pink, Mountain	*Aspiring.*
Pink, Red, Double	*Pure and ardent love.*
Pink, Single	*Pure love.*
Pink, Variegated	*Refusal.*
Pink, White	*Ingeniousness. Talent.*
Plane Tree	*Genius.*
Plum, Indian	*Privation.*
Plum Tree	*Fidelity.*
Plum, Wild	*Independence.*
Polyanthus	*Pride of riches.*
Polyanthus, Crimson	*The heart's mystery.*
Polyanthus, Lilac	*Confidence.*
Pomegranate	*Foolsihness.*
Pomegranate, Flower	*Mature elegance.*
Poplar, Black	*Courage.*
Poplar, White	*Time.*
Poppy, Red	*Consolation.*
Poppy, Scarlet	*Fantastic extravagance.*
Poppy, White	*Sleep, My bane. My antidote.*
Potato	*Benevolence.*

Prickly Pear . . . . *Satire.*
Pride of China . . . . *Dissension.*
Primrose . . . . *Early youth.*
Primrose, Evening . . . . *Inconstancy.*
Primrose, Red . . . . *Unpatronized merit.*
Privet . . . . *Prohibition.*
Purple Clover . . . . *Provident.*
Pyrus Japonica . . . . *Fairies' fire.*

Quaking-Grass	. . . .	*Agitation.*
Quamoclit	. . . .	*Busybody.*
Queen's Rocket	. . . .	*You are the queen of coquettes. Fashion.*
Quince	. . . .	*Temptation.*

Ragged Robin	*Wit.*
Ranunculus	*You are radiant with charms.*
Ranunculus, Garden	*You are rich in attractions.*
Ranunculus, Wild	*Ingratitude.*
Raspberry	*Remorse.*
Ray Grass	*Vice.*
Red Catchfly	*Youthful love.*
Reed	*Complaisance. Music.*
Reed, Split	*Indiscretion.*
Rhododendron (Rosebay)	*Danger. Beware.*
Rhubarb	*Advice.*
Rocket	*Rivalry.*
Rose	*Love.*
Rose, Austrian	*Thou art all that is lovely.*
Rose, Bridal	*Happy love.*
Rose, Burgundy	*Unconscious beauty.*
Rose, Cabbage	*Ambassador of love.*
Rose, Campion	*Only deserve my love.*
Rose, Carolina	*Love is dangerous.*
Rose, China	*Beauty always new.*
Rose, Christmas	*Tranquillize my anxiety.*

Rose, Daily	*Thy smile I aspire to.*
Rose, Damask	*Brilliant complexion.*
Rose, Deep Red	*Bashful shame.*
Rose, Dog	*Pleasure and pain.*
Rose, Guelder	*Winter. Age.*
Rose, Hundred-leaved	*Pride.*
Rose, Japan	*Beauty is your only attraction.*
Rose, Maiden Blush	*If you love me, you will find it out.*
Rose, Multiflora	*Grace.*
Rose, Mundi	*Variety.*
Rose, Musk	*Capricious beauty.*
Rose, Musk, Cluster	*Charming.*
Rose, Single	*Simplicity.*
Rose, Thornless	*Early attachment.*
Rose, Unique	*Call me not beautiful.*
Rose, White	*I am worthy of you.*
Rose, White (withered)	*Transient impressions.*
Rose, Yellow	*Decrease of love. Jealously.*
Rose, York and Lancaster	*War.*
Rose, Full-blown, placed over two Buds	*Secrecy.*
Rose, White and Red together	*Unity.*
Roses, Crown of	*Reward of virtue.*
Rosebud, Red	*Pure and lovely.*
Rosebud, White	*Girlhood.*
Rosebud, Moss	*Confession of love.*
Rosebay (Rhododendron)	*Beware. Danger.*
Rosemary	*Remembrance.*
Rudbeckia	*Justice.*
Rue	*Disdain.*
Rush	*Docility.*
Rye Grass	*Changeable disposition.*

Saffron	Beware of excess.
Saffron Crocus	Mirth.
Saffron, Meadow	My happiest days are past.
Sage	Domestic virtue.
Sage, Garden	Esteem.
Sainfoin	Agitation.
Saint John's Wort	Animosity. Superstition.
Sardony	Irony.
Saxifrage, Mossy	Affection.
Scabious	Unfortunate love.
Scabious, Sweet	Widowhood.
Scarlet Lychnis	Sunbeaming eyes.
Schinus	Religious enthusiasm.
Scotch Fir	Elevation.
Sensitive Plant	Sensibility. Delicate feelings.
Senvy	Indifference.
Shamrock	Light heartedness.
Snakesfoot	Horror.

Snapdragon	*Presumption.*
Snowball	*Bound.*
Snowdrop	*Hope.*
Sorrel	*Affection.*
Sorrel, Wild	*Wit ill-timed.*
Sorrel, Wood	*Joy.*
Southernwood	*Jest. Bantering.*
Spanish Jasmine	*Sensuality.*
Spearmint	*Warmth of sentiment.*
Speedwell	*Female fidelity.*
Speedwell, Germander	*Facility.*
Speedwell, Spiked	*Semblance.*
Spider, Ophrys	*Adroitness.*
Spiderwort	*Esteem not love.*
Spiked Willow Herb	*Pretension.*
Spindle Tree	*Your charms are engraven on my heart.*
Star of Bethlehem	*Purity.*
Starwort	*Afterthought.*
Starwort, American	*Cheerfulness in old age.*
Stock	*Lasting beauty.*
Stock, Ten Week	*Promptness.*
Stonecrop	*Transquillity.*
Straw, Broken	*Rupture of a contract.*
Straw, Whole	*Union.*
Strawberry Tree	*Esteem and love.*
Sumach, Venice	*Splendour. Intellectual excellence.*
Sunflower, Dwarf	*Adoration.*
Sunflower, Tall	*Haughtiness.*
Swallow-wort	*Cure for heartache.*
Sweet Basil	*Good wishes.*
Sweetbrier, American	*Simplicity.*
Sweetbrier, European	*I wound to heal.*
Sweetbrier, Yellow	*Decrease of love.*
Sweet Pea	*Delicate pleasures.*
Sweet Sultan	*Felicity.*
Sweet William	*Gallantry.*
Sycamore	*Curiosity.*
Syringa	*Memory.*
Syringa, Carolina	*Disappointment.*

Tamarisk	. . . .	*Crime.*
Tansy (Wild)	. . . .	*I declare war against you.*
Teasel	. . . .	*Misanthropy.*
Tendrils of Climbing Plants	.	*Ties.*
Thistle, Common	. . . .	*Austerity.*
Thistle, Fuller's	. . . .	*Misanthropy.*
Thistle, Scotch	. . . .	*Retaliation.*
Thorn Apple	. . . .	*Deceitful charms.*
Thorn, Branch of	. . . .	*Severity.*
Thrift	. . . .	*Sympathy.*
Throatwort	. . . .	*Neglected beauty.*
Thyme	. . . .	*Activity.*
Tiger Flower	. . . .	*For once my pride befriend me.*
Traveller's Joy	. . . .	*Safety.*
Tree of Life	. . . .	*Old age.*
Trefoil	. . . .	*Revenge.*

Tremella Nestoc	*Resistance.*
Trillium Pictum	*Modest beauty.*
Truffle	*Surprise.*
Trumpet Flower	*Fame.*
Tuberose	*Dangerous pleasures.*
Tulip	*Fame.*
Tulip, Red	*Declaration of love.*
Tulip, Variegated	*Beautiful eyes.*
Tulip, Yellow	*Hopeless love.*
Turnip	*Charity.*
Tussilage (Sweet-scented)	*Justice shall be done you.*

Valerian	An accommodating disposition.
Valerian, Greek	Rupture.
Venice Sumach	Intellectual excellence. Splendour.
Venus' Car	Fly with me.
Venus' Looking-glass	Flattery.
Venus' Trap	Deceit.
Vernal Grass	Poor, but happy.
Veronica	Fidelity.
Vervain	Enchantment.
Vine	Intoxication.
Violet, Blue	Faithfulness.
Violet, Dame	Watchfulness.
Violet, Sweet	Modesty.
Violet, Yellow	Rural happiness.
Virginian Spiderwort	Momentary happiness.
Virgin's Bower	Filial love.
Volkamenia	May you be happy.

Walnut	Intellect. Stratagem.
Wall-flower	Fidelity in adversity.
Water Lily	Purity of heart.
Water Melon	Bulkiness.
Wax Plant	Susceptibility.
Wheat Stalk	Riches.
Whin	Anger.
White Jasmine	Amiableness.
White Lily	Purity and Modesty.
White Mullein	Good nature.
White Oak	Independence.
White Pink	Talent.
White Poplar	Time.
White Rose (dried)	Death preferable to loss of innocence.
Whortleberry	Treason.
Willow, Creeping	Love forsaken.
Willow, Water	Freedom.

Willow, Weeping . . . . *Mourning.*
Willow-Herb . . . . *Pretension.*
Willow, French . . . . *Bravery and humanity.*
Winter Cherry . . . . *Deception.*
Witch Hazel . . . . *A spell.*
Woodbine . . . . *Fraternal love.*
Wood Sorrel . . . . *Joy. Maternal tenderness.*
Wormwood . . . . *Absence.*

Xanthium . . . . *Rudeness. Pertinacity.*
Xeranthemum . . . . *Cheerfulness under*
                                           adversity.

Yew . . . . *Sorrow*

Zephyr Flower . . . . *Expectation.*
Zinnia . . . . *Thoughts of absent friends.*

LANGUAGE OF FLOWERS.

Absence . . . . *Wormwood.*
Abuse not . . . . *Crocus.*
Acknowledgment . . . . *Canterbury Bell.*
Activity . . . . *Thyme.*
Admiration . . . . *Amethyst.*
Adoration . . . . *Dwarf Sunflower*
Adroitness . . . . *Spider Ophrys.*
Adulation . . . . *Cacalia.*
Advice . . . . *Rhubarb.*
Affection . . . . *Mossy Saxifrage.*
Affection . . . . *Pear.*
Affection . . . . *Sorrel.*
Affection beyond the grave . . . . *Green Locust.*
Affection, maternal . . . . *Cinquefoil.*
Affectation . . . . *Cockscomb Amaranth.*
Affectation . . . . *Morning Glory.*
Afterthought . . . . *Michaelmas Daisy.*
Afterthought . . . . *Starwort.*
Afterthought . . . . *China Aster.*
Agreement . . . . *Straw.*
Age . . . . *Guelder Rose.*
Agitation . . . . *Moving Plant.*
Agitation . . . . *Sainfoin.*
Alas! for my poor heart . . . . *Deep Red Carnation.*
Always cheerful . . . . *Coreopsis.*
Always lovely . . . . *Indian Pink (double).*
Ambassador of love . . . . *Cabbage Rose.*

Amiability . . . . *Jasmine.*
Anger . . . . *Whin.*
Animosity . . . . *St. John's Wort.*
Anticipation . . . . *Gooseberry.*
Anxious and trembling . . . . *Red Columbine.*
Ardour . . . . *Cuckoo Plant.*
Argument . . . . *Fig.*
Arts or artifice . . . . *Acanthus.*
Assiduous to please . . . . *Sprig of Ivy with tendrils.*
Assignation . . . . *Pimpernel.*
Attachment . . . . *Indian Jasmine.*
Audacity . . . . *Larch.*
Avarice . . . . *Scarlet Auricula.*
Aversion . . . . *China or Indian Pink.*

Bantering . . . . *Southernwood.*
Baseness . . . . *Dodder of Thyme.*
Bashfulness . . . . *Peony.*
Bashful shame . . . . *Deep Red Rose.*
Beautiful eyes . . . . *Variegated Tulip.*
Beauty . . . . *Party-coloured Daisy.*
Beauty always new . . . . *China Rose.*
Beauty, capricious . . . . *Lady's Slipper.*
Beauty, capricious . . . . *Musk Rose.*
Beauty, delicate . . . . *Flower of an Hour.*
Beauty, delicate . . . . *Hibiscus.*
Beauty, divine . . . . *American Cowslip.*
Beauty, glorious . . . . *Glory Flower.*
Beauty, lasting . . . . *Stock.*
Beauty, magnificent . . . . *Calla Æthiopica.*
Beauty, mental . . . . *Clematis.*
Beauty, modest . . . . *Trillium Pictum.*
Beauty, neglected . . . . *Throatwort.*
Beauty, pensive . . . . *Laburnum.*
Beauty, rustic . . . . *French Honeysuckle.*
Beauty, unconscious . . . . *Burgundy Rose.*
Beauty is your only attraction . . . . . *Japan Rose.*
Belle . . . . *Orchis.*
Be mine . . . . *Four-leaved Clover.*
Beneficence . . . . *Marshmallow.*
Benevolence . . . . *Potato.*
Betrayed . . . . *White Catchfly.*
Beware . . . . *Oleander.*
Beware . . . . *Rosebay.*
Blackness . . . . *Ebony Tree.*
Bluntness . . . . *Borage.*
Blushes . . . . *Marjoram.*
Boaster . . . . *Hydrangea.*
Boldness . . . . *Pink.*
Bonds . . . . *Convolvulus.*

Bonds of Affection . . . . *Gillyflower.*
Bravery . . . . *Oak Leaves.*
Bravery and humanity . . . . *French Willow.*
Bridal favour . . . . *Ivy Geranium.*
Brilliant complexion . . . . *Damask Rose.*
Bulk . . . . *Water Melon. Gourd.*
Busybody . . . . *Quamoclit.*
Bury me amid Nature's beauties . . . . *Persimon.*

Call me not beautiful . . . . *Rose Unique.*
Calm repose . . . . *Buckbean.*
Calumny . . . . *Hellebore.*
Calumny . . . . *Madder.*
Change . . . . *Pimpernel.*
Changeable disposition . . . . *Rye Grass.*
Charity . . . . *Turnip.*
Charming . . . . *Cluster of Musk Roses.*
Charms, deceitful . . . . *Thorn Apple.*
Cheerfulness in old age . . . . *American Starwort.*
Cheerfulness under adversity . . . . . *Chinese Chrysanthemum.*
Chivalry . . . . *Monkshood (Helmet Flower).*
Cleanliness . . . . *Hyssop.*
Coldheartedness . . . . *Lettuce.*
Coldness . . . . *Agnus Castus.*
Colour of my life . . . . *Coral Honeysuckle.*
Come down . . . . *Jacob's Ladder.*
Comfort . . . . *Pear Tree.*
Comforting . . . . *Scarlet Geranium.*
Compassion . . . . *Allspice.*
Concealed love . . . . *Motherwort.*
Concert . . . . *Nettle Tree.*
Concord . . . . *Lote Tree.*
Confession of love . . . . *Moss Rosebud.*
Confidence . . . . *Hepatica.*
Confidence . . . . *Lilac Polyanthus.*
Confidence . . . . *Liverwort.*
Confidence in Heaven . . . . *Flowering Reed.*
Conjugal love . . . . *Lime, or Linden Tree.*
Consolation . . . . *Red Poppy.*
Constancy . . . . *Bluebell.*
Consumed by love . . . . *Syrian Mallow.*
Counterfeit . . . . *Mock Orange.*
Courage . . . . *Black Poplar.*
Crime . . . . *Tamarisk.*
Cure . . . . *Balm of Gilead.*
Cure for heartache . . . . *Swallow-wort.*
Curiosity . . . . *Sycamore.*

Danger . . . . *Rhododendron. Rosebay.*
Dangerous Pleasures . . . . *Tuberose.*

Death . . . . *Cypress.*
Death preferable to loss of innocence . *White Rose (dried).*
Deceit . . . . *Apocynum.*
Deceit . . . . *Flytrap.*
Deceit . . . . *Dogsbane.*
Deceitful charms . . . . *Thorn Apple.*
Deception . . . . *White Cherry Tree.*
Declaration of love . . . . *Red Tulip.*
Decrease of love . . . . *Yellow Rose.*
Delay . . . . *Eupatorium.*
Delicacy . . . . *Bluebottle. Centaury.*
Dejection . . . . *Lichen.*
Desire to please . . . . *Mezereon.*
Despair . . . . *Cypress.*
Despondency . . . . *Humble Plant.*
Devotion . . . . *Peruvian Heliotrope.*
Difficulty . . . . *Blackthorn.*
Dignity . . . . *Cloves.*
Dignity . . . . *Laurel-leaved Magnolia.*
Disappointment . . . . *Carolina Syringa.*
Disdain . . . . *Yellow Carnation.*
Disdain . . . . *Rue.*
Disgust . . . . *Frog Ophrys.*
Dissension . . . . *Pride of China.*
Distinction . . . . *Cardinal Flower.*
Distrust . . . . *Lavender.*
Divine beauty . . . . *American Cowslip.*
Docility . . . . *Rush.*
Domestic industry . . . . *Flax.*
Domestic virtue . . . . *Sage.*
Durability . . . . *Dogwood.*
Duration . . . . *Cornel Tree.*
Early attachment . . . . *Thornless Rose.*
Early friendship . . . . *Blue Periwinkle.*
Early youth . . . . *Primrose.*
Elegance . . . . *Locust Tree.*
Elegance and grace . . . . *Yellow Jasmine.*
Elevation . . . . *Scotch Fir.*
Eloquence . . . . *Indian Lagerstræmia.*
Enchantment . . . . *Holly Herb.*
Enchantment . . . . *Vervain.*
Energy in adversity . . . . *Camomile.*
Envy . . . . *Bramble.*
Error . . . . *Bee Ophrys.*
Error . . . . *Fly Orchis.*
Esteem . . . . *Garden Sage.*
Esteem not love . . . . *Spiderwort.*
Esteem and love . . . . *Strawberry Tree.*
Estranged love . . . . *Lotus Flower.*
Excellence . . . . *Camellia Japonica.*

Expectation	*Anemone.*
Expectation	*Zephyr Flower.*
Expected meeting	*Nutmeg Geranium.*
Extent	*Gourd.*
Extinguished hopes	*Major Convolvulus.*
Facility	*Germander Speedwell.*
Fairies' fire	*Pyrus Japonica.*
Faithfulness	*Blue Violet.*
Faithfulness	*Heliotrope.*
Falsehood	*Burglass.*
Falsehood	*Yellow Lily.*
Falsehood	*Manchineal Tree.*
Fame	*Tulip. Trumpet Flower.*
Fame speaks him great and good . . .	*Apple Blossom.*
Fantastic extravagance	*Scarlet Poppy.*
Farewell	*Michaelmas Daisy.*
Fascination	*Fern.*
Fascination	*Honesty.*
Fashion	*Queen's Rocket.*
Fecundity	*Hollyhock.*
Felicity	*Sweet Sultan.*
Female fidelity	*Speedwell.*
Festivity	*Parsley.*
Fickleness	*Abatina.*
Fickleness	*Pink Larkspur.*
Filial love	*Virgin's bower.*
Fidelity	*Veronica. Ivy.*
Fidelity	*Plum Tree.*
Fidelity in adversity	*Wall-flower.*
Fidelity in love	*Lemon Blossoms.*
Fire	*Fleur-de-Luce.*
First emotions of love	*Purple Lilac.*
Flame	*Fleur-de-lis. Iris.*
Flattery	*Venus' Looking-glass.*
Flee away	*Pennyroyal.*
Fly with me	*Venus' Car.*
Folly	*Columbine.*
Foppery	*Cockscomb Amaranth.*
Foolishness	*Pomegranate.*
Foresight	*Holly.*
Forgetfulness	*Moonwort.*
Forget me not	*Forget Me Not.*
For once may pride befriend me	*Tiger Flower.*
Forsaken	*Garden Anemone.*
Forsaken	*Laburnum.*
Frankness	*Osier.*
Fraternal love	*Woodbine.*
Freedom	*Water Willow.*
Freshness	*Damask Rose.*

Friendship . . . . *Acacia.*
Friendship, early . . . . *Blue Periwinkle.*
Friendship, true . . . . *Oak-leaved Geranium.*
Friendship, unchanging . . . . *Arbor Vita.*
Frivolity . . . . *London Pride.*
Frugality . . . . *Chicory. Endive.*

Gaiety . . . . *Butterfly Orchis.*
Gaiety . . . . *Yellow Lily.*
Gallantry . . . . *Sweet William.*
Generosity . . . . *Orange Tree.*
Generous and devoted affection . . . . . *French Honeysuckle.*
Genius . . . . *Plane Tree.*
Gentility . . . . *Corn Cockle.*
Girlhood . . . . *White Rosebud.*
Gladness . . . . *Myrrh.*
Glory . . . . *Bay Tree.*
Glory . . . . *Laurel.*
Glorious beauty . . . . *Glory Flower.*
Goodness . . . . *Bonus Henricus.*
Goodness . . . . *Mercury.*
Good education . . . . *Cherry tree.*
Good wishes . . . . *Sweet Basil.*
Goodnature . . . . *White Mullein.*
Gossip . . . . *Cobæa.*
Grace . . . . *Multiflora Rose.*
Grace and elegance . . . . *Yellow Jasmine.*
Grandeur . . . . *Ash Tree.*
Gratitude . . . . *Small White Bell-flower.*
Grief . . . . *Harebell.*
Greif . . . . *Marigold.*

Happy love . . . . *Bridal Rose.*
Hatred . . . . *Basil.*
Haughtiness . . . . *Purple Larkspur.*
Haughtiness . . . . *Tall Sunflower.*
Health . . . . *Iceland Moss.*
Hermitage . . . . *Milkwort.*
Hidden worth . . . . *Coriander.*
Honesty . . . . *Honesty.*
Hope . . . . *Flowering Almond.*
Hope . . . . *Hawthorn.*
Hope . . . . *Snowdrop.*
Hope in adversity . . . . *Spruce Pine.*
Hopeless love . . . . *Yellow Tulip.*
Hopeless, not heartless . . . . *Love Lies Bleeding.*
Horror . . . . *Mandrake.*
Horror . . . . *Dragonwort.*
Horror . . . . *Snakesfoot.*
Hospitality . . . . *Oak Tree.*

Humility . . . . *Broom.*
Humility . . . . *Small Bindweed.*
Humility . . . . *Field Lilac.*

I am too happy . . . . *Cape Jasmine.*
I am your captive . . . . *Peach Blossom.*
I am worthy of you . . . . *White Rose.*
I change but in death . . . . *Bay Leaf.*
I declare against you . . . . *Belvedere.*
I declare against you . . . . *Liquorice.*
I declare war against you . . . . *Wild Tansy.*
I die if neglected. . . . . *Laurestina.*
I desire a return of affection . . . . . . *Jonquil.*
I feel my obligations . . . . *Lint.*
I feel your kindness . . . . *Flax.*
I have lost all . . . . *Mourning Bride.*
I live for thee . . . . *Cedar Leaf.*
I love . . . . *Red Chrysanthemum.*
I partake of your sentiments . . . . . *Double China Aster.*
I partake your sentiments . . . . *Garden Daisy.*
I shall die to-morrow . . . . *Gum Cistus.*
I shall not survive you . . . . *Black Mulberry.*
I surmount difficulties . . . . *Mistletoe.*
I will think of it . . . . *Single China Aster.*
I will think of it . . . . *Wild Daisy.*
I wound to heal . . . . *Eglantine (Sweetbrier).*
If you love me, you will find it out . . . *Maiden Blush Rose.*
Idleness . . . . *Mesembryanthemum.*
Ill-natured beauty . . . . *Citron.*
Imagination . . . . *Lupine.*
Immortality . . . . *Amaranth (Globe).*
Impatience . . . . *Yellow Balsam.*
Impatient of absence . . . . *Corchorus.*
Impatient resolves . . . . *Red Balsam.*
Imperfection . . . . *Henbane.*
Importunity . . . . *Burdock.*
Inconstancy . . . . *Evening Primrose.*
Incorruptible . . . . *Cedar of Lebanon.*
Independence . . . . *Wild Plum Tree.*
Independence . . . . *White Oak.*
Indifference . . . . *Everflowering Candytuft.*
Indifference . . . . *Mustard Seed.*
Indifference . . . . *Pigeon Berry.*
Indifference . . . . *Senvy.*
Indiscretion . . . . *Split Reed.*
Industry . . . . *Red Clover.*
Industry, Domestic . . . . *Flax.*
Ingeniousness . . . . *White Pink.*
Ingenuity . . . . *Pencilled Geranium.*
Ingenuous simplicity . . . . *Mouse-eared Chickweed.*

Ingratitude .... *Crowfoot.*
Innocence .... *Daisy.*
Insincerity .... *Foxglove.*
Insinuation .... *Great Bindweed.*
Inspiration .... *Angelica.*
Instability .... *Dahlia.*
Intellect .... *Walnut.*
Intoxication .... *Vine.*
Irony .... *Sardony.*

Jealousy .... *French Marigold.*
Jealousy .... *Yellow Rose.*
Jest .... *Southernwood.*
Joy .... *Wood Sorrel.*
Joys to come .... *Lesser Celandine.*
Justice .... *Rudbeckia.*
Justice shall be done to you ...... *Coltsfoot.*
Justice shall be done to you ...... *Sweet-scented Tussilage.*

Knight-errantry .... *Helmet Flower (Monkshood).*

Lamentation .... *Aspon Tree.*
Lasting beauty .... *Stock.*
Lasting pleasures .... *Everlasting Pea.*
Let me go .... *Butterfly Weed.*
Levity .... *Larkspur.*
Liberty .... *Live Oak.*
Life .... *Lucern.*
Lightheartedness .... *Shamrock.*
Lightness .... *Larkspur.*
Live for me .... *Arbor Vitæ.*
Love .... *Myrtle.*
Love .... *Rose.*
Love, forsaken .... *Creeping Willow.*
Love, returned .... *Ambrosia.*
Love is dangerous .... *Carolina Rose.*
Lustre .... *Aconite-leaved Crowfoot, or Fair Maid of France.*
Luxury .... *Chesnut Tree.*

Magnificent beauty .... *Calla Æthiopica.*
Majesty .... *Crown Imperial.*
Malevolence .... *Lobelia.*
Marriage .... *Ivy.*
Maternal affection .... *Cinquefoil.*
Maternal love .... *Moss.*
Maternal tenderness .... *Wood Sorrel.*
Matrimony .... *American Linden.*
May you be happy .... *Volkamenia.*
Meanness .... *Cuscuta.*

Meekness	Birch.
Melancholy	Dark Geranium.
Melancholy	Dead Leaves.
Mental beauty	Clematis.
Mental beauty	Kennedia.
Message	Iris.
Mildness	Mallow.
Mirth	Saffron Crocus.
Misanthropy	Aconite (Wolfsbane).
Misanthropy	Fuller's Teasel.
Modest beauty	Trillium Pictum.
Modest genius	Creeping Cereus.
Modesty	Violet.
Modesty and purity	White Lily.
Momentary happiness	Virginian Spiderwort.
Mourning	Weeping Willow.
Music	Bundles of Reed with their panicles.
My best days are past	Colchicum, or Meadow Saffron
My regrets follow you to the grave	Asphodel.
Neatness	Broom.
Neglected beauty	Throatwort.
Never-ceasing remembrance	Everlasting.
Old age	Tree of Life.
Only deserve my love	Campion Rose.
Painful recollections	Flos Adonis.
Painting	Auricula.
Painting the lily	Daphne Odora.
Passion	White Dittany.
Paternal error	Cardamine.
Patience	Dock. Ox Eye.
Patriotism	American Elm.
Patriotism	Nasturtium.
Peace	Olive.
Perfected loveliness	Camellia Japonica, White.
Perfidy	Common Laurel, in flower.
Pensive beauty	Laburnum.
Perplexity	Love in a Mist.
Persecution	Chequered Fritillary.
Perseverance	Swamp Magnolia.
Persuasion	Althea Frutex.
Persuasion	Syrian Mallow.
Pertinacity	Clotbur.
Pity	Pine.
Pleasure and pain	Dog Rose.
Pleasure, lasting	Everlasting Pea.

Pleasures of memory	*White Periwinkle.*
Popular favour	*Cistus, or Rock Rose.*
Poverty	*Evergreen Clematis.*
Power	*Imperial Montague.*
Power	*Cress.*
Precaution	*Golden Rod.*
Prediction	*Prophetic Marigold.*
Pretension	*Spiked Willow Herb.*
Pride	*Amaryllis.*
Pride	*Hundred-leaved Rose.*
Privation	*Indian Plum.*
Privation	*Myrobalan.*
Profit	*Cabbage.*
Prohibition	*Privet.*
Prolific	*Fig Tree.*
Promptness	*Ten-week Stock.*
Prosperity	*Beech Tree.*
Protection	*Bearded Crepis.*
Prudence	*Mountain Ash.*
Pure love	*Single Red Pink.*
Pure and ardent love	*Double Red Pink.*
Pure and lovely	*Red Rosebud.*
Purity	*Star of Bethlehem.*
Quarrel	*Broken Corn-straw.*
Quicksightedness	*Hawkweed.*
Reason	*Goat's Rue.*
Recantation	*Lotus Leaf.*
Recall	*Silver-leaved Geranium.*
Reconciliation	*Filbert.*
Reconciliation	*Hazel.*
Refusal	*Striped Carnation.*
Regard	*Daffodil.*
Relief	*Balm of Gilead.*
Relieve my anxiety	*Christmas Rose.*
Religious superstition	*Aloe.*
Religious superstition	*Passion Flower.*
Religious enthusiasm	*Schinus.*
Remembrance	*Rosemary.*
Remorse	*Bramble.*
Remorse	*Raspberry.*
Rendezvous	*Chickweed.*
Reserve	*Maple.*
Resistance	*Tremella Nestoc.*
Restoration	*Persicaria.*
Retaliation	*Scotch Thistle.*
Return of happiness	*Lily of the Valley.*
Revenge	*Birdsfoot Trefoil.*
Reverie	*Flowering Fern.*

Reward of merit	*Bay Wreath.*
Reward of virtue	*Garland of Roses.*
Riches	*Corn.*
Rigour	*Lantana.*
Rivalry	*Rocket.*
Rudeness	*Clotbur.*
Rudeness	*Xanthium.*
Rural happiness	*Yellow Violet.*
Rustic beauty	*French Honeysuckle.*
Rustic oracle	*Dandelion.*
Sadness	*Dead Leaves.*
Safety	*Traveller's Joy.*
Satire	*Prickly Pear.*
Sculpture	*Hoya.*
Secret Love	*Yellow Acacia.*
Semblance	*Spiked Speedwell.*
Sensitiveness	*Mimosa.*
Sensuality	*Spanish Jasmine.*
Separation	*Carolina Jasmine.*
Severity	*Branch of Thorns.*
Shame	*Peony.*
Sharpness	*Barberry Tree.*
Sickness	*Anemone (Zephyr Flower).*
Silliness	*Fool's Parsley.*
Simplicity	*American Sweetbrier.*
Sincerity	*Garden Chervil.*
Slighted love	*Yellow Chrysanthemum.*
Snare	*Catchfly. Dragon Plant.*
Solitude	*Heath.*
Sorrow	*Yew.*
Sourness of Temper	*Barberry.*
Spell	*Circæa.*
Spleen	*Fumitory.*
Splendid beauty	*Amaryllis.*
Splendour	*Austurtium.*
Sporting	*Fox-tail Grass.*
Stedfast Piety	*Wild Geranium.*
Stoicism	*Box Tree.*
Strength	*Cedar. Fennel.*
Submission	*Grass.*
Submission	*Harebell.*
Success crown your wishes	*Coronella.*
Succour	*Juniper.*
Sunbeaming eyes	*Scarlet Lychnis.*
Surprise	*Truffle.*
Susceptibility	*Wax Plant.*
Suspicion	*Champignon.*
Sympathy	*Balm.*
Sympathy	*Thrift.*

Talent . . . . *White Pink.*
Tardiness . . . . *Flax-leaved Goldy-locks.*
Taste . . . . *Scarlet Fuchsia.*
Tears . . . . *Helenium.*
Temperance . . . . *Azalea.*
Temptation . . . . *Apple.*
Thankfulness . . . . *Agrimony.*
The colour of my fate . . . . *Coral Honeysuckle.*
The heart's mystery . . . . *Crimson Polyanthus.*
The perfection of female loveliness . . *Justicia.*
The witching soul of music . . . . . . *Oats.*
Thoughts . . . . *Pansy.*
Thoughts of absent friends . . . . *Zinnia.*
Thy frown will kill me . . . . *Currant.*
Thy smile I aspire to . . . . *Daily Rose.*
Ties . . . . *Tendrils of Climbing Plants.*
Timidity . . . . *Amaryllis.*
Timidity . . . . *Marvel of Peru.*
Time . . . . *White Poplar.*
Tranquillity . . . . *Mudwort.*
Tranquillity . . . . *Stonecrop.*
Tranquillize my anxiety . . . . *Christmas Rose.*
Transient beauty . . . . *Night-blooming Cereus.*
Transient impressions . . . . *Withered White Rose.*
Transport of joy . . . . *Cape Jasmine.*
Treachery . . . . *Bilberry.*
True love . . . . *Forget Me Not.*
True Friendship . . . . *Oak-leaved Geranium.*
Truth . . . . *Bittersweet Nightshade.*
Truth . . . . *White Chrysanthemum.*

Unanimity . . . . *Phlox.*
Unbelief . . . . *Judas Tree.*
Unceasing remembrance . . . . *American Cudweed.*
Unchanging friendship . . . . *Arbor Vitæ.*
Unconscious beauty . . . . *Burgundy Rose.*
Unexpected meeting . . . . *Lemon Geranium.*
Unfortunate attachment . . . . *Mourning Bride.*
Unfortunate love. . . . . *Scabious.*
Union . . . . *Whole Straw.*
Unity . . . . *White and Red Rose
together.*
Unpatronized merit . . . . *Red Primrose.*
Uselessness . . . . *Meadowsweet.*
Utility . . . . *Grass.*

Variety . . . . *China Aster.*
Variety . . . . *Mundi Rose.*
Vice . . . . *Darnel (Ray Grass).*
Victory . . . . *Palm.*

Virtue . . . . *Mint.*
Virtue, Domestic . . . . *Sage.*
Volubility . . . . *Abecedary.*
Voraciousness . . . . *Lupine.*
Vulgar Minds . . . . *African Marigold.*

War . . . . *York and Lancaster Rose.*
War . . . . *Achillea Millefolia.*
Warlike trophy . . . . *Indian Cress.*
Warmth of feeling . . . . *Peppermint.*
Watchfulness . . . . *Dame Violet.*
Weakness . . . . *Moschatel.*
Weakness . . . . *Musk Plant.*
Welcome to a stranger . . . . *American Starwort.*
Widowhood . . . . *Sweet Scabious.*
Win me and wear me . . . . *Lady's Slipper.*
Winning grace . . . . *Cowslip.*
Winter . . . . *Guelder Rose.*
Wit . . . . *Meadow Lychnis.*
Wit ill-timed . . . . *Wild Sorrel.*
Witchcraft . . . . *Enchanter's Nightshade.*
Worth beyond beauty . . . . *Sweet Alyssum.*
Worth sustained by judicious and
tender affection . . . . *Pink Convolvulus.*
Worthy all praise . . . . *Fennel.*

You are cold . . . . *Hortensia.*
You are my divinity . . . . *American Cowslip.*
You are perfect . . . . *Pine Apple.*
You are radiant with charms . . . . . . *Ranunculus.*
You are rich in attractions . . . . *Garden Ranunculus.*
You are the queen of coquettes . . . . *Queen's Rocket.*
You have no claims . . . . *Pasque Flower.*
You please all . . . . *Branch of Currants.*
You will be my death . . . . *Hemlock.*
Your charms are engraven on
my heart . . . . *Spindle Tree.*
Your looks freeze me . . . . *Ice Plant.*
Your presence softens my pains . . . . *Milkvetch.*
Your purity equals your loveliness . . *Orange Blossoms.*
Your qualities, like your charms,
are unequalled . . . . *Peach.*
Your qualities surpass your charms . . *Mignionette.*
Youthful innocence . . . . *White Lilac.*
Youthful love . . . . *Red Catchfly.*

Zealousness . . . . *Elder.*
Zest . . . . *Lemon.*

ILLUSTRATIONS